Crazy Book of
Practical Jokes

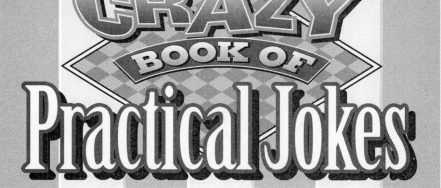

Crazy Book of Practical Jokes

with Glen Singleton

Crazy Book of Practical Jokes
First published in 2003 by Hinkler Books Pty Ltd
17–23 Redwood Drive
Dingley VIC 3172 Australia
www.hinklerbooks.com

ISBN: 186515685X

Cover designer: Peter Tovey Studios
Editor: Rose Inserra
Typesetting: Midland Typesetters
Printed and bound in Australia

Introduction

Playing practical jokes is great fun. Part of the fun comes from planning the joke and thinking about the end result. The rest of the fun comes from seeing the joke work. For a practical joke to work, there has to be a victim. The victim is the person the practical joke is played on. Some practical jokes have more than one victim. Whenever you carry out a practical joke, remember these two important rules.

- Practical jokes should never hurt anyone.

- Practical jokes should never be cruel.

This book contains some crazy practical jokes. Each joke is divided into two main sections: the Sting and the Set-up. The Sting describes what happens to the victim in the

1

joke. When a practical joke is successfully played on someone, it is said that they have been 'stung'. The Set-up explains how to set-up and carry out the joke.

Remember when playing a practical joke that a victim often seeks revenge. Don't play practical jokes unless you are willing to take them as well.

Just one more tip before you start. Never play a practical joke on someone who you know will not take it in good spirit. Practical jokes are meant to be fun.

Warning: Some of the practical jokes in this book require adult supervision. Children should never climb a ladder, use a knife or scissors, or use a sewing needle without an adult being present. A practical joke is never worth doing if either the person carrying out the joke or the intended victim risk injury.

No Joke

This practical joke involves not playing a practical joke, which makes it a very good practical joke indeed. Does that make sense?

The Sting

It is traditional to play practical jokes on people on 1 April—April's Fool Day.

April Fool's Day is approaching. Every year, you have played a practical joke on a particular victim. This year, the victim again expects to have a practical joke played on them. You remind them that April Fool's Day is approaching and they start getting worried. On the morning of April Fool's Day, they wake up in a sweat, dreading what's going to happen today. Until midday, when April Fool's Day officially ends, they cannot relax for a second. When midday passes, they breathe a big sigh of relief because they haven't been a victim of a practical joke. At least that's what they think. The fact that you didn't play a practical joke was a joke in itself because you had them so worried.

The rabbit who wouldn't eat his carrots as a child...

What You Need

- nothing, just a victim

The Set-up

1. As April Fool's Day approaches, pick a victim who would expect you to play a joke on them.

2. Every day, remind them how many days it is until April Fool's Day.

3. Tell them that you have a really big practical joke planned for them this year.

4. The day before April Fool's Day, walk past them rubbing your hands together, as if you are getting really excited about the joke you are going to play the following day.

5. On the morning of April Fool's Day, walk past them several times and chuckle or give them a grin. This will make them feel even more uncomfortable.

6. At one minute to midday on Aprils Fool's Day, walk up to the victim and say 'April Fool'.

7. When the victim reminds you that April Fool's Day ends in one minute and that you have not played a joke on them, tell them that you've been playing the joke all morning. Explain that the joke was the fact you didn't play a joke, but you still managed to have them running scared.

The Disappearing Money

Everyone loves finding money in the street. Particularly when the money is a note. This joke gets people excited about finding money. The problem is, they can't grab hold of it.

The Sting

The victim of the joke is walking down the street. They notice a piece of paper in the middle of the footpath. It looks like money but they can't be sure from a distance. As they get closer, they realise that they're right. They can't believe their luck. They think about what they're going to buy with the money. They bend down to pick it up, and just before they grab it, it skips away. Even if they chase the money, it keeps skipping away every time they get close to it.

What You Need

- a money note

- some fishing line

- a large bush, tree, fence or wall to hide behind

The Set-up

1. Make a tiny hole in the note and thread some fishing line through it.

2. Pick a place where there is a bush, tree, fence or wall that you can hide behind. Make sure that you have a good view of the footpath, but that people walking along the footpath cannot see you.

3. When no one is coming, place the note on the footpath, then hide.

4. Hold the end of the fishing line and wait for a victim.

5. When someone bends down to pick up your note, jerk the fishing line so that the note moves away from the victim.

6. Keep doing this for as long as the person chases the note.

Set-up Tip

- You have to be very alert while you're doing this joke. Otherwise you may lose your money. Apart from running the risk of someone picking the note up before you have time to jerk the fishing line, you have to watch out for people using a foot to trap the money. If they stamp on the note before you pull the line, the note will stay under their shoe. Then you'll be the victim.

Similar Joke

- A similar joke can be done with a coin. Instead of using fishing line, use extra-strength glue to stick the coin to the footpath. Then stand back and watch people struggle to pick it free. The only problem with this joke is that you won't get your coin back.

Buzzing Balloons

If you blow up a balloon and tie a knot in the end, you have something you can kick and hit. If you blow up a balloon and don't tie a knot in the end, you have something that can whiz and buzz around a room.

The Sting

The victim of the joke is about to walk into a room. Everything seems normal and they do not suspect that they are about to have a practical joke played on them. All that changes as they turn the doorknob and open the door. As the door opens, a balloon whizzes around the room, giving the victim a nasty scare. They have no idea where the balloon came from. And if you don't tell them, they never will know.

What You Need

- a balloon

- a door and doorframe

The Set-up

1. Blow up a balloon. Do not tie a knot in the end of the balloon.

2. Place the end of the balloon between the door and the doorframe, so that the balloon is held in place and is not losing air. You may have to try various doors and doorframes before you find a suitable one.

3. Close the door and wait for your victim to open the door.

4. If you want to make a really big impact, place a few balloons in the door. The more you have, the bigger the buzz.

5. Stand back and watch the look on your victim's face as they open the door and the balloon you positioned between the door and doorframe is suddenly released. It will start to whiz about. Your victim won't be able to work out what's going on.

Similar Jokes

- Place a bucket of water on top of a slightly open door. Make sure that the bucket is fastened to something so that it tips when the door opens, but does not fall. You do not want a full bucket of water dropping on someone's head.

- Place a bag full of flour on top of a slightly open door. When the victim opens the door, the bag will fall on their head, causing a great mess. Make sure the bag is not too heavy. You don't want to knock anyone out.

- Balance a row of ping-pong balls along the top of a slightly open door. When the victim pushes the door, the balls will fall all over the place.

Holding the String

You can play this joke on one or two people. Either way, it's fun. The length of the joke depends on how long it takes before the victim realises they have been the target of a practical joker.

The Sting

The victim is walking along the footpath. You are standing nearby with a ball of string, a ruler and other measuring equipment. You are looking rather flustered. As the victim passes, you approach them and ask if they would mind holding one end of the string for a minute while you take the other end around the corner to do some measuring. The victim agrees. They stand still, holding the string. They wait for a couple of minutes and you have not returned. They are getting impatient, but they keep holding the string for a bit longer. Finally, they have had enough and they go looking for you. They turn the corner and you are nowhere to be seen.

What You Need

- a ball of string

- some measuring equipment

- a corner block

The Set-up

1. Set up your equipment on a corner block. You have to make sure that the person you ask to hold the string will not be able to see around the corner.

2. Other than the ball of string, it doesn't really matter what your other measuring

equipment is. It's only there for show,
to look as if you are doing some serious
measuring.

3. When your victim approaches, ask them if
   they could help you for a minute. Tell them
   that you are doing a school project and
   that you have to measure from the point
   where they are standing to another point
   just around the corner.

4. Pick up your measuring equipment and
   take the other end of the string around
   the corner, where the victim can no longer
   see you.

5. Tie the end of the string to a fence or gate.
   If you may want to fool another person,
   ask someone else to hold the end of the
   string and tell them that you have to check
   a measurement around the next corner.

6. Leave the scene. You can go home and
   wonder how long the victim or victims
   waited for, or you can hide somewhere
   and watch how long it takes them to
   realise they have been stung.

CD Swap

This joke will frustrate your victim. It is especially good to play this joke on people who are particular about the way they organise their CD collection.

The Sting

The victim goes to put on one of their favourite CDs. They turn the CD player on, take the CD out of its cover and put it in the player. They press the 'Play' button and get a shock when the music that plays is not what they expected. They take the CD out and check the label. It does not match the cover. They grab another CD from their collection and look inside. This one is also wrong. They go through their entire collection and every single CD has been swapped around.

What You Need

- the victim's CD collection

- about half an hour to do the swapping

The Set-up

1. Make sure the victim is occupied elsewhere for at least half an hour.

2. Stack the CD covers into one large pile. Do not take the CDs out of their covers yet.

3. Open the top CD cover and take the CD out. Open the second CD cover and take the CD out. Place the first CD into the second CD cover.

4. Open the third CD cover and take the CD out. Place the second CD into the third CD cover.

5. Repeat this process right to the bottom of the pile. The last CD will go in the top CD cover. (The reason for swapping the CDs in such an organised manner is to ensure that no CD is put back into its own cover.)

6. Put the CDs back where you got them from. If the victim always has their CDs in a certain order, make sure that you put them back in the same order. Otherwise they'll suspect someone has touched them.

Similar Jokes

- You can also play this joke with people's video collections and vinyl record collections.

- You can swap people's books around by swapping the dust covers on their books. To make things even worse for the victim, put some of the dust covers on upside down.

'Look, Up in the Sky'

This joke costs nothing, needs no equipment and can have many victims. That makes it a very good practical joke to play.

The Sting

A crowd of people is gathered at the bottom of a tall building. Everyone is looking up at the top of the building. Some of the people start whispering and asking each other what is going on. Over the next few minutes, the crowd grows bigger and bigger. Rumours start spreading that someone is out on the roof of the building. After about ten minutes, the crowd has become so large that it is holding up traffic. A police officer comes along and tells the crowd to move away. Eventually, the crowd does move away. Many of them watch the television news that night to see if anything dramatic happened. Of course, the incident doesn't make it to the news because nothing did happen. It was all a practical joke started by you.

What You Need

- a tall building in a busy street

- a couple of volunteers

The Set-up

1. Pick a tall building in a busy street.

2. When there are quite a few people walking past, stand at the bottom of the building and look up at the top.

3. Have one of your friends walk past and stop near you. You have to act as if you

don't know each other. Your friend should also look up.

4. Have another friend walk past and stop. Again, you should all act as if you don't know each other. One of you should point towards the top of the building and whisper something to the others.

5. By now, you should have aroused the interest of people passing by.

6. As the crowd of people grows, you and your friends should walk away and watch from somewhere else.

Similar Jokes

- If you are on a crowded beach, look at the sea and point out into the distance.

- If you are at a sporting event, stand up and look at a point several rows behind you.

- If you are in the classroom, look out of the window and point into the distance.

Cool Confetti

In this joke, confetti rains on people when they are inside a room. It can only be played on hot days when people are seeking a little cool relief. Your classroom would be a great place to play the Cool Confetti practical joke.

The Sting

A class full of children is waiting for their teacher to arrive. They are yelling loudly and running around. It is a warm day and everyone is getting a bit hot. The teacher arrives and tells everyone to be quiet and to sit in their seats. The teacher then notices that the overhead fan is not on, so the teacher switches it on. The blades of the fan slowly start to spin around. As the speed of the blades increases, confetti starts to rain down on everyone. The schoolchildren scream with delight, and the teacher can do nothing but watch as more and more colourful confetti falls from the blades and is swept throughout the room by the draught made by the fan.

What You Need

- a room with an overhead, spinning fan

- confetti

- a stepladder or desk and chair

- an adult to help

The Set-up

1. Make sure that it is a hot day. If you play this trick in the middle of winter, you'll be

waiting months before anyone turns the fan on.

2. Pick a room where there is an overhead fan with wide blades.

3. Make sure the fan is turned off.

4. Climb to the top of the stepladder or place a chair on top of a table and carefully climb onto the chair.

5. Get an adult to hold the stepladder or chair for you. They should also make sure that no one walks into the room and turns the fan on.

6. Pour the confetti on top of the fan blades and spread it around.

7. Get down and hide the stepladder or put the table and chair back in place.

8. Wait for someone to turn the fan on, then watch as it starts raining confetti.

Similar Jokes

You don't have to put confetti on top of the fan blades. There are other items you can use. Here are a few suggestions:

- crumpled pieces of paper

- toy plastic flies or plastic spiders (to give people a fright)

- balloons that have been blown up just a tiny bit

Whatever you use, make sure that it won't hurt anyone when it falls from the fan.

Making an Impression

This practical joke leaves quite a mark on your victim! And sometimes the victim can walk around for ages before realising they've been stung in a practical joke.

The Sting

You and the victim are playing a game with some coins. You persuade the victim to try and stick a coin to their forehead. They do so. When they take the coin away, they are left with a dark impression of the coin. Even though everyone else can see the impression of the coin, the victim is unaware that they have been stung.

What You Need

- two coins

- a felt pen or some powder

The Set-up

1. Fill in one side of a coin with the felt pen or cover it with powder. Make-up powder is very good for this purpose.

2. Stand in front of your victim and press the coin that is not marked onto your forehead.

3. When your victim asks what you are doing, tell them that you heard on the radio that people who can stick coins to their forehead are supposed to be smarter than those who can't. Your victim will probably want to have a go, so that they can prove how smart they are.

4. Tell the victim that you'll show them exactly where the coin has to go. Then, take the coin that has the marked side and press that side firmly in the middle of the victim's forehead. Make sure the victim does not see the marks or powder.

5. Tell the victim to hold the coin firmly in place for two minutes. After two minutes, tell the victim to let go.

6. If the coin is stuck to the forehead, pull the coin off and tell them that they are obviously very intelligent.

7. If the coin falls off, grab it and put it in your pocket. Tell them that you couldn't make the coin stick either. This will make them feel better.

8. Whether the coin sticks or falls, the victim will have an impression of the coin stuck on their forehead and they will walk around without realising it.

Name That Tune

Some tunes are nice to hear once or twice. After a few hearings, they can begin to get on your nerves. After many, many hearings they start to drive you mad. This practical joke drives people mad.

The Sting

The victim is sitting in the lounge relaxing. They are reading a book and do not want to be disturbed. Suddenly, they hear a tune. They ignore it, hoping it will go away. A few minutes later, they notice the tune is still playing. Now they are having trouble concentrating on their book and they are not as relaxed as they were. After ten minutes, they get up to find where the tune is coming from. It seems to be coming from inside a cupboard. They open the cupboard door and begin to rummage through the contents. The tune is still playing. Finally, at the back of the cupboard, they discover a small device playing the tune. By now, the floor is full of stuff they have thrown out of the cupboard and they are feeling anything but relaxed.

What You Need

- a musical birthday card

- a room with a hiding place

The Set-up

1. Buy a musical birthday card.

2. Take the musical chip out of the card.

3. Pick a hiding place, such as a cupboard, in your classroom, at home, or in an office or

store. Make sure the hiding place is near where your victim sits.

4. When you know your victim is on their way, set the musical chip off and put it in the hiding place.

5. Leave the scene.

Similar Joke

- While going on a long family holiday in the car, set a musical chip off and put it down the back of a seat or somewhere else it cannot be easily reached. It will drive everyone mad (though it might drive you mad as well).

Changing Room

Have you ever had the urge to move all the furniture in your bedroom, just for a change of scenery? Well, it's much more fun if you do it to a friend's room — without them knowing.

The Sting

The victim goes to their bedroom after being away for the day. They open the bedroom door and cannot believe their eyes. Their bed is where the desk usually is, and the desk is where the bed usually is. The posters that were on the walls are now on the ceiling, and the rug from the floor is hanging over the curtain rod. The clothes that were hanging in the wardrobe have been squashed into the chest of drawers, and the socks, underpants and handkerchiefs that were in the chest of drawers are now on hangers in the wardrobe.

What You Need

- a friend's bedroom

- some friends to help you

- about half a day

- an adult

The Set-up

1. Get permission from the victim's parents to change the victim's bedroom around. (You will probably have to promise to help the victim put everything back where it was.)

2. Find out when the victim will be away from home for a few hours.

3. Make a plan at least a day before the joke. Draw a map of the victim's bedroom and work out where you are going to put everything.

4. Write down the order in which you are going to move things. This will make things much easier on the day.

5. On the day of the joke, start work as soon as the victim leaves home. You may need all the time you can get.

6. Make sure you have a few friends to help you lift and move the items around.

7. When you have finished, leave a note on the bed with a message for the victim to work out. It could be the name of a furniture-

NON RETURNABLE
BOOMERANG
GUARANTEED - NOT TO
COME BACK EVERY TIME

moving service made up of the first letters of everyone who helped play the joke.

Safety Tip

- Lifting heavy objects can cause injuries. Make sure that an adult is helping you.

Leaves, Leaves, Leaves

Have you ever wondered what to do with the piles of leaves that collect under trees? Well, here's one idea that will bring a smile to your face.

The Sting

The victim wakes up in the morning and gets ready for work. They have a shower, eat breakfast and say goodbye to their family. They open the front door and go to step outside. But they can't take a single step because they are faced with the largest pile of leaves they have seen in their life. They have to push and shove the leaves out of the way before they can make their way outside. At the end of the day, when they return home, they find a huge pile of leaves again blocks their front door. This time they can't get into their house without pushing the leaves away.

What You Need

- lots and lots of leaves

- garbage bags

- a chair or stepladder

The Set-up

1. Collect as many leaves as you can from your garden. You can even offer to rake up your neighbours' gardens so you can get more leaves.

2. Pack all the leaves into garbage bags.

3. Get up early before the victim is out of bed and take the garbage bags full of leaves to the victim's house. Empty one of the bags before the front door.

4. Empty a second bag on top of the pile, and then empty a third bag and a fourth bag.

5. By now you will probably need the chair or stepladder to reach the top of the pile.

6. Hide somewhere so that you can see the reaction on the victim's face when they open the front door.

7. You could also do this joke while your victim is out during the day, or repeat it in the afternoon so they are 'stung' twice.

Set-up Tip

- Do not attempt this joke when it is windy, otherwise the leaves will just blow away before the victim comes across the pile.

Similar Joke

- If you live in an area that gets hit by snowstorms in winter, you could shovel huge piles of snow instead of leaves.

Holiday Snaps

This joke takes some organising but it is very funny. Some people use garden gnomes to play this joke, but you can use your victim's favourite toy or other item.

The Sting

The victim gets an envelope in the mail. They open it up and inside is a photograph of their favourite teddy bear at the airport. On the back of the photo is a note saying 'You never take me anywhere so I've gone on a trip by myself'. The victim races up to their room to look for their teddy bear. They can't find it anywhere. Over the next few weeks, they receive lots of photos of their teddy bear at various holiday destinations. One morning, just as they begin to wonder whether they will ever see their teddy bear again, they open the front door to find their teddy bear on the doormat. The bear is holding a note saying 'I'm back. Did you miss me?'

What You Need

- a toy or favourite item from the victim

- a camera

- envelopes

- stamps

- someone going on a holiday

The Set-up

1. Find someone who is going on a holiday and is willing to help you play this joke. If you are going on holiday, you can do it

yourself, but the victim may guess that you're playing a practical joke on them. It is best if the victim does not know the person on holiday.

2. Sneak one of the victim's favourite toys out of their room. Don't worry, they will get it back. A doll, teddy bear or other soft toy is best.

3. Give the toy to the person going on holiday.

4. Also give the person going on holiday your victim's address and a few envelopes. If the person is having a holiday within your country, you can give them the stamps they'll need. If the person is going overseas, they will have to buy the stamps themselves. You can give them some money to pay for the stamps.

5. Instruct the person going on holiday to position the toy in front of famous landmarks and take photos of the toy.

6. They should then write a message on the back of each photo and send the photos to the victim.

7. When the person returns from holiday, get the toy back and place it outside the victim's front door.

Glitter from Above

This joke requires a fair bit of setting up and testing but it's well worth the effort. It will take the victim ages to get rid of all the glitter that has fallen on them.

The Sting

The victim sits down at their desk to do a bit of homework. They get their books ready and take their pens and pencils out of their pencil case. Before starting, they decide to sharpen their pencils. They open the desk drawer where they keep their pencil sharpener.

A moment later, a pile of glitter falls from the ceiling and onto their head, their books and all over the carpet. What a mess!

What You Need

- a white handkerchief

- glitter or confetti

- fishing line

- pins or sticky tape

- a desk with a drawer

- a ladder

- a couple of hours to set up and test the joke

- an adult to help

The Set-up

1. Make a small hole in the middle of one of the edges of the handkerchief.

2. Tie one end of the fishing line to the hole.

3. Fill the handkerchief with glitter.

4. Position the ladder so that you can reach the ceiling above the victim's desk chair. Ask an adult to help you.

5. Climb the ladder and lightly pin or tape the four corners of the handkerchief to the ceiling.

6. The fishing line will be dangling from the handkerchief. Lightly tape it in a couple of places so that it sticks to the ceiling and the wall. You do not want it dangling in view.

7. Tie the free end of the fishing line to the back of the top drawer of the desk.

8. The victim opens the drawer, tugging on the fishing line. This pulls the handkerchief away from the ceiling. The glitter falls on the victim's head.

9. You will probably have to practise this a number of times to make sure that you have not attached the handkerchief too tightly to the ceiling.

The Holey Cup

Watch the frustration as your thirsty victim tries their best to quench their thirst, only to end up with the contents of their drink down the front of their shirt.

The Sting

The victim of the joke gets ready to drink something delicious. Imagine how frustrated they get when the liquid leaks out of the cup and onto their clothes before it reaches their mouth.

What You Need

- a plastic cup

- a pin

- a tasty drink

- a cloth

The Set-up

1. Use the pin to prick some holes just below the rim of the cup.

2. Tempt the victim with the offer of a tasty drink.

3. Pour the drink but make sure that the liquid remains below the pinholes.

4. Give the victim the drink.

5. Watch as the drink spurts out of the holes before it can reach the victim's mouth.

6. Use the cloth to help the victim clean themselves up.

Set-up Tips

- Make sure that the holes in the cup are large enough for liquid to flow through but small enough so that the victim cannot see them.

- Practise the joke with water before your victim is at your house. That way you can make sure the holes are exactly the right size.

- Know what your victim's favourite drink is. That way they'll find your offer of a drink hard to refuse.

The Holey Straw

This practical joke is similar to the Holey Cup joke, except that it is a straw that causes the problem.

The Sting

Like the Holey Cup joke, the victim of the joke gets ready to drink something delicious. This time, their frustration comes about because they cannot suck any liquid up through their straw. No matter how hard they suck on the straw, all that happens is their face gets redder and redder.

What You Need

- a straw

- a pin

- a cup or can of tasty drink

The Set-up

1. Use the pin to prick two holes near the bottom of the straw and two more near the top of the straw. The holes should be opposite each other.

2. Give the victim the drink. It is best if it is a drink that you know they like. That way they'll find it hard to refuse.

3. Watch as they try to suck the drink up through the straw. The holes make it virtually impossible for liquid to make its way up the straw.

4. Encourage the victim to suck harder. Then enjoy the discomfort they are experiencing.

Follow-up

- You could have a second holey straw handy. Then you could tell the victim that there must be something wrong with the first straw and offer them the replacement. Watch with delight as they struggle again.

The Goldfish

Play this joke on a friend who has a goldfish.
It's amazing how much a carrot can look like
a goldfish.

The Sting

The victim of the joke is very proud of their
goldfish. Every time you go around to their
house, they show it to you. This time, as they
show it to you, you mention how hungry you
are. The victim goes into the kitchen to find
something to eat and you follow. They have
their back turned to you, but they hear you

mumble with your mouth full, 'It's too late.
I couldn't help myself. I was just so hungry.'
They turn and scream, as they see the tail of
their goldfish hanging out the end of your
mouth. You take one big gulp and the tail
disappears as well.

What You Need

- a carrot

- a sharp knife

- a victim with a goldfish

- an adult to help

The Set-up

1. Get a carrot.

2. Ask an adult to carefully cut the ends off
   the carrot. They need to carve the thick
   part of the carrot in the shape of a
   goldfish tail. (They don't have to carve the
   carrot into the shape of a whole goldfish,
   as your victim will only see the piece
   hanging out of your mouth.)

3. Next time you go over to the victim's house put the carved carrot into your pocket.

4. When the victim shows you their goldfish, make a comment about how hungry you are.

5. If the victim does not show you their goldfish, ask to see it, then make a comment about how hungry you are.

6. As you follow your victim into the kitchen, pull the carrot out of your pocket. Then place it in your mouth, with the tail piece hanging out.

7. Make a loud, mumbling comment about not being able to wait.

8. After you've chewed and swallowed the 'tail', say, 'Goldfish aren't nearly as bad as I thought they'd be'. Then ask, 'Have you got any more?'

Smelly House

This joke takes a while to become effective, but once it does, it stinks! And one of the best parts of this joke is that by the time the victim realises they've been 'stung', you are long gone and they have no idea who played the joke on them.

The Sting

The victim does not notice anything is wrong, at first. However, over the next few days they notice a smell in their living room. They assume that the smell will go away, but it doesn't. It just gets worse. Finally, the smell gets so bad that the victim tries to find where it's coming from. They get down on their hands and knees and, using their nose, they try to sniff it out. When they have no luck, they stand on a chair and try to sniff it out. Finally, they track the smell to the curtain behind the sofa. They look behind the curtain find some cheese, getting older, mouldier and smellier by the minute.

What You Need

- some cheese, fish or other smelly food

- an open container to put the food in

The Set-up

1. Buy some smelly cheese, a small bit of fish or some other type of smelly food. It should be fresh when you buy it, so that it does not smell straight away. You want the smell to develop slowly over a few days or even a couple of weeks. That will make it even more irritating for the victim.

2. Put the food in an open container and hide the container in a place where it cannot be easily seen. If the victim has a pet, do not leave it on the ground. Otherwise the pet will eat it and the joke will not work. Apart from behind a curtain, other good hiding places are underneath the sofa (taped to the bottom), on top of a cupboard, behind a row of books on the bookshelf, and behind a stereo system.

3. Don't let on that you can smell anything until the victim mentions it. Otherwise they may get suspicious and figure out that it was you who planted the food.

4. If you really want to make an impression, you could plant food in different places throughout the victim's house. But you'd better not let them know who did it. They might make you eat the rotten food when they've found it all.

Set-up Tip

- You don't have to plant the food in someone's house. The back of the car is a good place. So is your classroom.

Sugar and Salt

This is one of the oldest jokes around. It's an easy way to play havoc with someone's taste buds.

The Sting

The victim sits down to a nice hot cup of coffee. They've been working hard and looking forward to this drink all day. They grab the sugar container and pour sugar into their cup. They then stir the liquid and take a sip. Imagine their horror when their coffee tastes of salt instead of sugar.

What You Need

- a sugar container

- a salt container

- two saucers

The Set-up

1. Grab the salt and sugar containers at your victim's house.

2. Place the two saucers in front of you.

3. Pour the contents of the sugar container onto one saucer.

4. Pour the contents of the salt container onto the other saucer.

5. Pour the sugar from the saucer into the salt container.

6. Pour the salt from the saucer into the sugar container.

7. Put the containers back where you found them.

8. Try and be there when the victim gets a taste sensation they are not expecting.

9. This is a particularly good joke to play in a school cafeteria. Tell a few of your friends what you have done and have a laugh together as someone pours the wrong substance on their food or in their drink.

What a Mess

This joke can be played with salt, pepper and sugar containers.

The Sting

The victim sits down to have breakfast. They pour some cereal into a bowl and add their milk. They then grab the sugar container and turn it upside down so that the sugar sprinkles onto their cereal. However, as soon as the sugar container is upside down, the lid falls off and the entire contents of the container pour on top of their cereal.

What You Need

- a salt, sugar or pepper container with a screw-top lid

The Set-up

1. Take the salt, pepper or sugar container and unscrew the lid until it is right off.

2. Place the lid on top of the container. It should look as if it is sitting on the container properly, but it is really not attached at all.

3. Put the container back in place. When someone goes to use it, the lid will come right off when they turn it upside down.

The Bottomless Cup

This joke involves sugar and a sugar container. A laugh is guaranteed, as is a mess.

The Sting

The victim has just woken up and made their way to the kitchen. They are still a bit sleepy. They get the breakfast cereal out of the cupboard, the milk out of the fridge and a clean bowl and spoon from the dishwasher. They sit down at the breakfast table, pour the cereal into their bowl and add a splash of milk. They then decide to sprinkle a bit of sugar on top of the cereal. The sugar is in a plastic cup, not a container. They reach for the plastic cup and lift it towards them. The sugar pours all over the table, making a huge mess. The victim turns the cup upside down to see that it has no bottom.

What You Need

- a plastic cup (not a clear one)

- a pair of scissors

- sugar

The Set-up

1. Cut the bottom out of the plastic cup. Do not put a lid on the cup because you want the victim to see that it has sugar inside. However, you do not want a clear plastic cup, as they might notice it does not have a bottom.

2. Position the cup where the victim will find it. Once the sugar is in the cup, you will not be able to move it.

3. Pour the victim's sugar from their sugar container into the plastic cup.

4. Hide the victim's real sugar container. (Don't worry about the victim becoming suspicious that the sugar is in a different container. They will probably think that someone broke the other container or that it is dirty.)

5. Leave the room and wait for the cry when the victim picks the cup up.

6. Alternatively, you could make sure you are in the kitchen when you know the victim will use the sugar. That way you'll see the action first hand.

Similar Jokes

This practical joke is not restricted to sugar. You can cut the bottom out of any cheap plastic, cardboard or paper container. Here are a few suggestions:

- cereal packets
- bags of sugar

- bags of flour

- bags of rice

Don't cut the bottom out of a container full of liquid. The liquid will just spill out before you get to play the joke.

Jelly Juice

This joke will really frustrate anyone who is very thirsty and wants a drink of juice. No matter how much they shake the bottle, the juice just won't come out.

The Sting

The victim is very thirsty. They go to the fridge and take out a bottle of juice. They get a glass from the cupboard and unscrew the lid from the bottle. They then tip the bottle and try to pour the juice into the glass. The only problem is that the juice won't come out.

They can see the juice inside, but it just won't flow. They have a good look inside the bottle. There's nothing blocking the juice. They try once more, then give up and have a glass of water instead.

What You Need

- a bottle of juice
- an empty container
- some jelly

The Set-up

1. Take a bottle of juice.

2. Pour the juice into an empty container and keep it to drink later.

3. Following the instructions on the jelly packet, make the jelly mixture in the juice bottle. (Make sure that the colour of the jelly is the same as the colour of the juice.)

4. Hide the bottle in the back of the fridge to set.

5. When the jelly has set, put the bottle where the juice usually is.

6. Wait for the victim to grab the bottle, then walk past and enjoy the look of frustration on their face.

Similar Jokes

- Rather than replace the juice with jelly, you could put the bottle in the freezer and return it to the fridge when the juice has frozen. The victim won't be able to get a drink of juice this way either.

A Little Extra

One of the best things about 'A Little Extra' is that there can be a number of victims.

The Sting

The whole family is sitting down for their evening meal. It's their favourite, spaghetti bolognaise. The bowl of spaghetti is handed around and everyone serves themselves. Then the bolognaise sauce is handed around and everyone scoops some out and pours it on top of their spaghetti. It smells so good. After the cheese is added, they tuck into their meal. The first person to swallow a mouthful screams and runs to the water tap. Suddenly, a second person follows. Then a third and a fourth. The bolognaise sauce has been tampered with and is so spicy that no one can eat it.

What You Need

- a hot, spicy food additive

- a water supply where the meal is served

The Set-up

1. Get hold of a hot, spicy food additive. There may be some in your kitchen cupboard. Otherwise, you'll have to buy the additive from the store. Below are a few examples of the type of additive you can use:

   - curry powder

   - paprika

   - chilli powder

- pepper

- tabasco sauce

2. Take out the additive when someone is cooking a spaghetti sauce or a stew or casserole. These are ideal meals to add an additive to because the additive will usually blend in and not be noticed until it is tasted.

3. When the cook leaves the kitchen, sneak in and pour your additive into the food. Stir it very well, then leave the cooking implements exactly as they were when the cook left the kitchen.

4. When the dinner is served and the victims start reaching for water, do the same. That way you won't be suspected of having played the joke.

Set-up Tips

- Never play this joke if one of the possible victims is allergic to the food additive you are going to add. You do not want to make someone sick.

- The best day to play this joke is when you feel like takeaway food. When the joke takes effect, it will be too late to cook another meal, so the whole family will have to get takeaway.

- Many cooks taste their creations as they are cooking. If this is the case with your cook, then you are going to have to add the hot, spicy additive just before the meal is served.

Movie Munchies

This joke may seem a little bit revolting, but you actually don't do anything revolting at all. It's all about planting an idea in the victim's mind.

The Sting

The victim, a friend of yours, is sitting at the movies. The advertisements and trailers have just finished and the main feature is about to start. The lights go out. You offer the victim a box of Maltesers, saying you are too full to finish them. The victim accepts and eats one of them. You then say something that makes the victim think twice about eating the rest of the Maltesers. It also spoils their enjoyment of the film. What is it that you say? Read the Set-up to find out.

What You Need

- a movie theatre

- a box of Maltesers, Jaffas, Kool Mints or other round, smooth sweets

The Set-up

1. Make sure you are sitting next to the victim in the movie theatre.

2. When the lights are completely out, hand over an opened box of Maltesers, Jaffas, Kool Mints or other round, smooth sweets.

3. Tell the victim that you are too full to eat them.

4. Wait until the victim has eaten one or two of the sweets and then say to the victim,

'By the way, I put one of the sweets up my nose and then put it back in the box'.

5. You haven't really put a sweet up your nose but the victim doesn't know this. They have to decide whether to believe you or not.

6. As the victim has already eaten a couple of the sweets, they will probably feel sick thinking that one of them could have been up your nose.

7. If they decide to eat the rest of the box, they will feel very uneasy throughout the movie. It is amazing how slimy these sweets feel when you have been told that one of them has been up someone's nose.

Four and Out

This joke almost always works. It is quick and easy and makes the victim kick themselves for being made a fool of so easily.

The Sting

You tell the victim that they won't be able to give incorrect answers to four questions. Of course, the victim claims that they can easily give four incorrect answers. How easy it seems to them. They give an incorrect answer to the first question. Then they give an incorrect answer to the second question. Then they give an incorrect answer to the third question. One question to go and they are feeling very confident indeed. You throw in a comment that requires them to answer. They give a correct answer without realising that this is the fourth question.

What You Need

- nothing, except a victim

The Set-up

1. Tell your victim that you bet they can't give an incorrect answer to four questions you're going to ask them. They'll probably be so confident that you can bet them some money or get them to be your servant for a day if they fail the task.

2. Make the first question an easy one. Something like 'Are you a boy?' To give the incorrect answer, boys would answer 'No' and girls would answer 'Yes'. If they give the correct answer, then you've won your bet already.

3. Make the second question another easy one or even a silly one. Something like 'Am I your grandparent?' They should answer 'Yes', as this is the incorrect answer. If they answer 'No', you've won.

4. The third question can also be easy. Ask them what day of the week it is. If they answer with today's day, you've won. If they answer with the wrong day, they're still in the contest. They're probably also feeling very confident.

WASH DAY AT THE OCTOPUS' PLACE

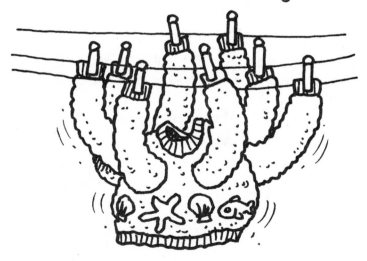

5. Now, instead of asking the fourth question like the previous ones, say 'That's three questions I've asked now, isn't it?' They will not expect that this is the fourth question and will answer 'Yes'. You then tell them that they have answered the fourth question correctly and have therefore lost the bet.

New Screensaver

Here's an opportunity to make your mark on someone else's computer, without doing any lasting damage. If your victim's confused enough, they even think their entire computer has been replaced.

The Sting

The victim of this joke leaves their computer for a few minutes to get something to eat, answer the phone, or for another reason. When they return, their normal screensaver has disappeared and been replaced by one that has a message saying 'You have been stung by [Your Name]' or 'I have gobbled up your screensaver', or by a humorous image.

An owl with laryngitis

What You Need

• the victim's computer

• three minutes alone with the computer

The Set-up

1. Make sure the victim is distracted for at least three minutes. Perhaps arrange for one of your friends to ring the victim at a particular time, when both you and your victim are at the victim's house.

2. Click the Start button on the computer taskbar.

3. Move the cursor to the Settings tag.

4. Click on Control Panel. The Control Panel box should open up.

5. Click on the icon that reads Display. The Display Properties box should open up.

6. There should be a tag that reads Screen Saver. Press on this tag. It allows you to change the screensaver.

7. There is a box that contains a list of all the possible screensavers. Press on the arrow to the left of this box to bring up the choices. Select one, then press Apply.

8. If you choose Scrolling Marquee, then Settings, a box comes up allowing you to type in a message. This message will scroll across the screen when the screensaver is activated.

9. Close all the boxes so that the computer looks exactly the way it did before you touched it.

Similar Joke

You can also change the amount of time it takes for the screensaver to appear. Why not change the time to one minute, so that if the computer is idle for this short period, the screensaver will pop up. The victim will start getting very annoyed indeed.

The Dusty Phone

This joke is really only appropriate if the victim has a cord phone, with the receiver connected to the handset.

The Sting

The victim gets a phone call from a representative of the telephone company. The victim is told that in ten minutes time, the telephone lines are going to be cleared of dust. To prepare for this, the victim is told to leave the phone off the hook and put a bag over the receiver so that it collects any dust that blows out of the holes and doesn't wreck the victim's carpet.

What You Need

- the telephone number of your victim

- someone who can pose as the representative of the telephone company, without laughing and without being recognised by the victim

The Set-up

1. Make sure you know when your victim will be home alone. You want them to answer the phone.

2. Ring up (or get someone else to ring up) and introduce yourself as a representative of the telephone company in your area.

3. Tell the victim that the company is currently cleaning the telephone lines in their district. This is done by blasting air through the lines to clear any dust. In ten

minutes time, it will be the turn of the victim's line.

4. Instruct the victim to leave the phone off the hook and to put a bag over the receiver. This will stop dust ruining the victim's carpet.

5. Thank the victim, then hang up.

6. Laugh as you imagine your victim standing next to the phone, waiting for the air to be blasted through the line.

Set-up Tips

- It is very important that the person posing as the telephone company representative sound as convincing as possible. They'll need to have answers ready for any questions that the victim might ask, such as 'How long will I need to keep the bag over the phone?' and 'What sort of equipment do you use to clear the lines?'

- Make sure the person posing as the telephone company representative knows the name of the victim and refers to them by that name. Otherwise the victim may guess that it is a joke. After all, the telephone company would have their name.

Follow-up

- If you believe that the victim is going to follow your instructions, ring them back about ten minutes later and tell them that the telephone company engineers discovered a new form of dust that is invisible to the human eye. Tell them to dispose of the bag carefully, being sure not to let any of the dust escape because it could cause a massive carpet stain in forty-eight hours time.

- You could also ring back, thank the victim for their cooperation and tell them that the process will be repeated at exactly the same time over the next three days. They may not have collected any dust today, but they probably will on one of these other occasions. Tell them to set an alarm so that they do not forget to put a bag over the receiver.

Collecting Your Messages

This joke can be played on someone answering the phone or to an answering machine.

The Sting

The victim gets a phone call from someone asking for Joe Bloggs (or any other name). The victim explains that the caller must have the wrong number because Joe Bloggs does not live there. Not long after, another caller rings and asks for Joe Bloggs. This continues a number of times. The victim is getting more and more heated up. Finally, someone rings up and says, 'Hi, it's Joe Bloggs here. Have you got any messages for me?'

What You Need

- the telephone number of your victim

- a number of people who can pose as callers without being recognised by the victim

The Set-up

1. Ring up the victim and ask to speak to Joe Bloggs (or any other name other than the victim's).

2. At last an hour later, get a second person to ring up and ask to speak to Joe Bloggs (or the other name).

3. At last another hour later, get a third person to ring up and ask to speak to Joe Bloggs.

4. At last another hour later, get a fourth person to ring up and ask to speak to Joe Bloggs (or the other name).

5. When you have had as many different people as possible ring up, make another call. This time, say 'Hello, this is Joe Bloggs (or the other name). Are there any messages for me?'

Set-up Tips

• Make sure you have a lot of people willing to ring up and ask for Joe Bloggs. You do not want to repeat callers, otherwise the victim will realise someone is playing a joke on them.

• This joke can be over in a couple of hours or it can drag on for weeks. You can have your callers ring the victim one after the other, before you ring up claiming to be Joe Bloggs. Or you can arrange it so that the victim receives a call every day or two for a few weeks, before you ring up claiming to be Joe Bloggs.

- Try to get your callers to each say something different, rather than all ringing up and asking 'Is Joe Bloggs there?' For example, one could be a telemarketer trying to sell something to Joe Bloggs. Another could be Joe's mother trying to get hold of him. Yet another could be a debt collector chasing Joe because he owes them money. The more variety, the better the joke.

- Of course, if the victim turns out to have the same name as the person you are leaving messages for, then you're going to have to do some pretty quick thinking.

The cat that made off with the mouse... and the computer

Follow-up

- If you know the victim's address as well as their phone number, you could send a few letters to Joe Bloggs, after you have finished with the telephone joke. Then ring the victim up a few days later and claim to be Joe Bloggs again. Ask the victim if they have any mail for you.

Emergency Call

This joke involves leaving a message on an answering machine. It does not work if someone answers the phone. Before ringing, make sure that your victim is out and that they have an answering machine. You can play this joke on a friend without disguising who you are.

The Sting

The victim gets home and sees they have a message on their answering machine. They press the 'Play' button and hear a message that says, 'Paula, [insert the victim's name instead] are you there? It's Jill [insert your name instead]. Please answer the phone if you're home. I need your help urgently. I think there's someone in my house and they're about to . . .' The message then cuts off.

What You Need

- the telephone number of your victim

- a victim with an answering machine

The Set-up

1. Make sure you know when there is going to be no-one home at your victim's house.

2. Ring up and put on a panicky voice, as if you are in trouble.

3. Start yelling for them to answer the phone, making it seem as if the danger is getting closer.

4. Finally, gasp for breath and hang-up in mid-sentence.

Set-up Tips

- You do not want your victim to panic and call the police after hearing your call. To avoid this, leave them another message immediately after the first. In this message, just say 'Paula, it's Jill. Only joking.'

- If you know when your victim is likely to get home, you could hide near their house and sneak to their front door when they go inside. Then listen for the phone message. As soon as it finishes, knock on the door. When they answer, say 'Surprise', or dress yourself up in torn clothes and fake blood.

Similar Joke

- Rather than scare the victim, you can frustrate them by ringing up and leaving a message saying, 'Hi Paula, it's Jill. You won't believe this. I just got offered two free tickets to [the name of a concert or sports event that you know the victim would love to attend]. The problem is they have to be picked up within the next half an hour and I can't get away from what I'm doing. If you want one of the tickets, ring me up by 4.30 and I'll tell you where to pick them up. It's just around the corner from your place. If you're later than 4.30, don't bother calling. The tickets will have gone.' Of course, you have to know that your friend will be away for at least half an hour.

The Phantom Telephone

This joke doesn't involve an actual phone. However, it does involve the sound of a telephone ringing. It's designed to drive someone mad. The Phantom Telephone joke works best if the victim does not have a cordless phone.

The Sting

Your victim decides that they should do some gardening. They put on their gardening clothes and boots and go into the garden. They've been outside for a couple of minutes when they hear the telephone ringing. They take off their boots and go inside. As soon as they get in the door, the phone stops ringing. They go outside again and put their boots back on. After five minutes of gardening, they hear the telephone ringing again. They run for the door, take off their muddy boots and step inside. As soon as they do, the phone stops ringing again. This happens three or four times and your victim gets angrier and angrier each time.

What You Need

- a tape recorder

- the victim's telephone

The Set-up

1. At least a day before you are going to play the joke, set your tape recorder up next to the victim's telephone.

2. Make sure that your victim is not in the house. If they see what you are doing, they will get suspicious.

3. Using a mobile phone, ring the number of the main phone. If you do not have a mobile phone, arrange for one of your friends to ring the number at a particular time.

4. While the phone is ringing, press the 'Record' button on your tape recorder and tape the ringing.

5. On the day of the joke, set the tape recorder up near the telephone. It has to appear as if the sound is coming from the phone. However, make sure that you and the tape recorder are hidden from view in case the victim makes it into the room.

6. Turn the volume of the tape recorder right up so that the victim will hear the ringing.

7. Wait until your victim is outside or is busy somewhere in the house. Then press the 'Play' button on your tape recorder.

8. As soon as the victim gets near the phone, turn the tape recorder off.

9. Rewind the tape and get ready to play the joke again.

10. Your victim doesn't have to be gardening for this joke to work. You can wait until they are doing almost any activity. Here are a few suggestions:

- when the victim is washing the car

- when the victim is outside practising their golf swing

- when the victim is having a bath

- when the victim is doing homework

Strange Perfume

This joke is one to play on your mother, or even your big sister, just before they start getting ready for a special night out. If they don't notice that something's wrong, anyone who gets close enough to them certainly will.

The Sting

Your victim is getting ready for a special night out. They've had a bath or shower, they've dressed in a brand new outfit and they've put their make-up on. There's just one thing left. They have to put some of their new perfume on. They twist the lid off the perfume bottle and dab a little of the perfume on. Then they go out. So far they haven't realised that anything is wrong. It's only when someone comments that they smell of vinegar that they realise they've been the target of a practical joke.

What You Need

- a bottle of the victim's perfume

- some vinegar

- a clean, empty perfume container

The Set-up

1. Make sure that your mother (or big sister) is not around.

2. Unscrew the lid of their perfume bottle and pour the perfume into the clean container.

3. Fill the real perfume bottle with vinegar.

4. Screw the lid back on and put the perfume bottle back where it is normally kept.

5. Put the container with the real perfume somewhere safe. When the joke is over, the victim will want their real perfume back. Perfume is very expensive and they are not going to be very happy if you have thrown it away.

6. Wait for the victim to put their perfume on and see if they notice the switch.

Set-up Tips

• If the victim notices that their perfume has been switched, give them the real perfume back so that they can finish getting ready and go out.

• If the victim does not notice that their perfume has been switched, you may want to tell them before they leave the house. Otherwise, you may ruin their night.

• If you let the victim go out wearing the vinegar perfume, go back into their room and switch the liquids around again. To do this, pour the vinegar down the sink, rinse the perfume bottle, then pour the real perfume back in. The victim will never know why they smelt of vinegar instead of perfume.

A New Outfit

The time to play this joke is when you've spotted a great shirt, pair of pants or skirt in a shop. You can't afford to buy it yourself and you doubt your parents will buy it for you. But if this joke is successful, the chances are you're going to have that new piece of clothing the same day.

The Sting

Your mother or father starts pulling wet clothes out of the washing machine. Suddenly they stop in shock. They pull out an item of your clothing that is ripped to shreds. It must have got caught up in one of the washing machine parts. When they show it to you, you get very upset. You may even burst into tears. You tell them it was your favourite item of clothing and that nothing could replace it. Then you suddenly remember that there is one item of clothing that could possibly replace it.

What You Need

- an old item of clothing

- a pair of scissors

- a washing machine

The Set-up

1. A few days before you play this joke, wear an old item of clothing and mention to your parents how much you like it. In reality, you should choose something you are not very keen on at all.

2. Wear the item of clothing at least once more over the next day or so.

3. When you're ready to play the joke, grab a pair of scissors and make a few small cuts in the piece of clothing.

4. Make the cuts larger by ripping them with your hands. This helps disguise the neat cuts made by the scissors.

5. Wait until one of your parents has put a load of washing into the washing machine. When they have turned the machine on and walked away, sneak in and put your item of clothing into the machine.

6. When your parent shows you the torn clothing, get very upset. Try and put on an Academy Award-winning acting performance.

7. When your parent tries to cheer you, mention the item of clothing that you saw in the shop. However, do not mention it too early or they may get suspicious.

Yesterday's News

Sometimes today's news seems very similar to yesterday's news. With this joke, today's news is *exactly the same* as yesterday's news.

The Sting

Your mother or father sits down to read the newspaper over breakfast. As they eat their cereal and drink their coffee, they read the front page. Then they read the second page. So far, they're reading the latest news. They go onto the third page, then the fourth page, and so on. The further they get into the newspaper, the more they begin to feel as if they've read it all before. They check the date on the front page, but it's certainly today's newspaper. So they go back to reading. Finally, they come across a story that they are sure they've read before. They check the date on that page. It's yesterday's date. Somehow, the inside pages of the newspaper are from the day before.

What You Need

- an old newspaper (preferably from the day before)

- today's newspaper

The Set-up

1. The day before you are going to play the joke, keep the newspaper after it has been read.

2. If you get the newspaper delivered to your house, get up nice and early on the day that you are going to play the joke so that you are the first to get to the paper.

3. If someone in your house usually goes to the shop to buy the newspaper, on the day that you are going to play the joke offer to go and buy it.

4. Take all of the inside pages out of today's newspaper. You should be left with the front and back pages, as well as the second and second last pages.

5. Take the inside pages out of yesterday's newspaper and place them inside the front and back pages of today's newspaper.

6. Put the newspaper in its usual place.

7. Sit near your parent as they read the newspaper. See how long it takes them to notice that they're reading yesterday's news.

Daylight Saving

Some states and countries turn their clocks
forward an hour at the beginning of summer
and turn them back again at the end of
summer. This is so people can enjoy more
sunshine at the end of the day, rather than
early in the morning when they are asleep.
This joke also involves changing the time on
clocks but it has nothing to do with daylight
saving.

The Sting

Your mother or father gets up in the morning
to get ready for work. They look at the clock

and notice that they have slept in. They have a quicker shower than usual, skip breakfast, race out of the house and rush to work. There seems to be less traffic than normal, which is good because it means they might not be too late for work. When they finally get to work, they find they're the first person there. They check their watch, then look at the clock at work. For some reason their watch is an hour faster than the clock.

What You Need

- all the clocks and watches in the house

The Set-up

1. Wait until your parents have gone to bed and are asleep.

2. Change the time on all the clocks in the house.

3. Also change the time on the your parents' watches. (Be very quiet when you're changing the time on the clocks and

watches in your parents' bedroom. You don't want to wake them.)

4. Some clocks are easy to overlook. You'll need to change these as well. These include:

- clocks on video recorders

- clocks on microwave ovens

- clocks on wall ovens

- clocks on computers

- clocks on radios

- clocks in cars

5. If you put the clocks forward, then your parents will think they're running late.

6. If you put the clocks back, then your parents will think they're running early.

7. Do not play this joke if one of your parents has an important meeting to attend. You do not want the joke to cause any major problems.

8. If you only want to cause minor inconvenience, change the time by half an hour instead of an hour.

9. If you have any brothers or sisters, tell them about the joke you are playing. That way, they won't spoil the joke by telling your parents the real time.

Burnt Toast

In most households the breakfast routine is the same every morning. This is a joke to play on someone who has toast for breakfast every morning. It is particularly good to play on someone who is very fussy about how they like their toast.

The Sting

Your mother or father turns the kettle on to boil water for their cup of tea or coffee. They also put two pieces of bread into the toaster. While their bread is toasting, they leave the kitchen to get their bag ready for work or to put a load of washing into the washing machine. When they return to the kitchen, their toast has popped up but it is burnt. The kitchen is full of smoke and the smoke alarm is ringing. Your parent checks the dial on the toaster but it is on its usual setting. They have no idea how their toast got burnt.

What You Need

- a toaster

The Set-up

1. Make sure that you get into the kitchen before anyone else.

2. Turn the dial on the toaster up so that it will heat the bread for longer than usual.

3. Do not act suspicious when your parent puts their toast in the toaster.

4. If your parent is out of the kitchen when their toast burns, quickly turn the dial back to its usual setting. This will confuse them even more.

5. If your parent stays in the kitchen, run to the toaster to rescue the burning toast. While you are there, quickly turn the dial back to its usual place.

6. Tell your parent that you heard on the radio that bakeries are slicing bread thinner than normal in a bid to put more slices into each packet. That must be the reason their toast burnt.

Similar Joke

- Rather than turning the dial up, you could turn the dial right down, so that the bread hardly toasts at all. When your parent goes to the toaster, they may even wonder whether they pushed the toaster lever down at all.

Bath Time

This is a great joke to play on your brother or sister. It works particularly well after they have had a tough day playing sport and are looking forward to a hot, relaxing bath.

The Sting

The victim runs a hot bath. They need it to soothe their tired muscles. When the bath is ready, they get undressed, step into the bath and lie down. The bottom of the bath feels scratchy. They move about in an attempt to get a bit more comfortable. But wherever they settle, it feels uncomfortable. Finally, they give themselves a quick wash and get out of the bath. It was far from satisfactory. They let the water out and notice a layer of sand on the bottom of the bath.

What You Need

- sand

- a bathtub

- a sibling who is really looking forward to having a bath

The Set-up

1. Buy or collect some sand. You don't need much. Hide it in a bag in a secret place.

2. Keep your ears and eyes open so that you know when your brother or sister is looking forward to having a bath.

3. Wait for them to run their bath.

4. While the water's running, they'll probably leave the bathroom. Sneak in

and sprinkle the sand into the bath. The sand will sink to the bottom. (Don't sprinkle in too much sand or the victim might notice it when they step into the bath. You want the victim to feel a little bit irritated by the sand while they're lying in the bath. You don't want them to put a foot straight into a pile of wet sand.)

5. Make sure that you're not around when the victim gets out of the bath. They'll probably be in a bad mood.

Similar Joke

- You can play a similar joke by squeezing a lot of bubble bath into the water while the bath is running. Make sure you squirt in a lot so that there are bubbles flowing over the side of the bath when the victim returns to the bathroom.

Wakey, Wakey

Don't play this joke on a brother or sister if you share a bedroom with them. Otherwise, the joke will be on you as well.

The Sting

It's four o'clock in the morning and your brother or sister is sound asleep. They had a late night and they went to bed looking forward to sleeping in. At four o'clock, their alarm clock goes off. It wakes them up. They're so sleepy that they try and think why they set the alarm to go off at four o'clock.

They can't think of any reason so they just turn the alarm clock off and go back to sleep. They never do find out why their alarm clock went off.

What You Need

- an alarm clock

- a tired brother or sister

- a torch (for Follow-up)

The Set-up

1. Before your brother or sister goes to bed, sneak into their room. (The best time to do this is when they are out with friends, watching their favourite TV show or having a bath or shower. This way it's unlikely you'll be seen.)

2. Set your brother's or sister's alarm clock to go off very early.

Follow-up

- If your brother or sister asks whether you played a joke on them, say 'No'. If you admit to playing the joke, they may try to get back at you.

- If you think that your brother or sister suspects you, make sure that you check your alarm clock before you go to sleep. They may try to play the same trick on you.

- If you are willing to get up early, you can continue the joke. Set your alarm to go off at the same time as your brother's or sister's alarm. Allow your brother or sister about fifteen minutes to get back to sleep, then sneak into their room. You may need a torch to see what you're doing. Set their alarm to go off again in an hour's time. Repeat this throughout the morning for as long as you think you can get away with it.

A Stitch in Time

This joke requires you to do a bit of sewing. You don't have to be a neat sewer because the victim will want to unpick your work straight away.

The Sting

Your brother or sister is getting ready to go out. They always take pride in their appearance. They get their clothes out of the cupboard and chest of drawers. They put their shirt on and try to put their arms through the sleeves. But their arms won't go through. The sleeves have been stitched together. They throw the shirt to the ground and put their trousers on. But their feet won't go through. The legs of the trousers have been stitched up as well. They realise that they've been the victims of a practical joke but there's no time to seek revenge now, they're too busy ripping the stitches out.

What You Need

- a needle and thread

- access to your victim's clothes

The Set-up

1. When your brother or sister is out, go to their room and get one of their shirts and one of their pairs of trousers.

2. Using the needle and thread, sew up the end of one of the sleeves.

3. Sew up the end of the other sleeve.

4. Sew up the end of one of the legs.

5. Sew up the end of the other leg.

6. Put the clothes back where you found it.

7. There are many items of clothing you could sew together. You could sew up the ends of their pyjamas or their school uniform. You could even sew the fingers on a pair of gloves together or the opening of a pocket. However, make sure

that you don't sew up any new or
expensive clothes.

Follow-up

* If your brother or sister has some friends
  around for a sleepover, sneak in and take
  some of the clothes they are going to wear
  the next day. Then sew the ends of a few
  of them together.

Mirror, Mirror on the Wall

Snow White looked in the mirror and was told she was the fairest of all. When your brother or sister looks in the mirror, they will certainly not be the fairest of all.

The Sting

You tell your brother or sister they have strange spots on their face. The victim does not believe you. You tell them you are not joking. Still they do not believe you. In the end, you go and fetch a mirror so they can see for themselves. When you come back with the mirror, you hold it up in front of their face. They get the shock of their life when they see that you are right. Their face is covered with spots.

What You Need

- A portable mirror

- A felt pen

The Set-Up

1. Find a portable mirror that is large enough to show someone's full face.

2. Using the felt pen, put a few spots on the mirror. Make sure that you put the spots where someone's face will appear. To do this, hold the mirror in front of your face at about the same distance that you will hold it from the victim's face.

3. Rather than come out straight away and tell the victim that they have spots on their

face, give them a couple of strange looks. When they ask you 'What's wrong?' tell them, 'There's nothing wrong'. Then wait a minute and give them another strange look. This time when they ask, 'What's wrong?' tell them they have spots on their face.

4. When they say they don't believe you, or if they get up to have a look, offer to get a mirror for them. Get up and fetch the mirror before they have a chance to get to another mirror first.

5. Carry the mirror so that the victim cannot see the front of it.

6. When you hold the mirror up in front of their face, make sure you keep it very still. Otherwise the spots will move and the victim will become suspicious.

The Stirrer

You can play this joke whenever one of your parents' friends pops in for a cup of tea or coffee. But don't play it on the same person twice or they'll get suspicious.

The Sting

The victim accepts your offer of a cup of coffee. You bring them their cup and teaspoon, as well as the milk and sugar. The victim adds a bit of milk to the coffee, then takes the teaspoon and spoons some sugar into the cup. They then stir their coffee.

When they take the teaspoon out, they're left with only the handle—the bottom part has fallen off. They have no idea how it happened but they feel very embarrassed.

What You Need

- an old teaspoon

- some chewing gum

- a hot cup of tea or coffee

The Set-up

1. Buy an old teaspoon from a second-hand shop or use an old one from home. Make sure you don't use a valuable teaspoon or someone's favourite spoon because you are going to destroy it.

2. Grab the oval end of the teaspoon with one hand and hold the handle tightly with the other hand.

3. Wiggle the oval end until you feel it loosening. It will eventually break off.

4. When it has broken off, get a tiny piece of chewing gum and stick the two pieces back together. Make sure that the gum cannot be seen. You only need enough to stop the spoon breaking when it is picked up.

5. Give the victim the spoon with their hot drink. It has to be a hot drink because the heat will melt the gum.

6. As the victim stirs sugar or milk into their drink, tell them that the spoon is your favourite because a very special friend gave it to you. This will make them feel even worse when it breaks.

Similar Joke

- You can play this joke on a whole heap of people at once. If you know that your parents are going to host a dinner party, prepare several spoons in the way described above and make sure that they are set out on the table with the coffee and tea.

Storm in a Bathroom

A school toilet is one place where kids probably think they are safe from practical jokes. But you know better, don't you?

The Sting

The victim walks into a toilet stall in a school toilet. This should be a good friend of yours. You could start a fight if it's someone who doesn't like you already. As soon as they have closed and locked the door, the lights flicker on and off and they hear someone yell out, 'Lightning, Lightning'. A moment later, they hear the sound of banging and someone yells out, 'Thunder, Thunder'. They get ready to leave the stall but it's too late. Someone yells out, 'Rain' and a moment later they are drenched after being hit by water coming over the top of the door.

What You Need

- a school toilet

- the light switch

- a bucket

- some water (clean water)

- a hot day

The Set-up

1. Pick a busy time, like lunch.

2. Fill the bucket with water.

3. Wait until the victim goes in to a stall and closes the door.

4. Switch the lights on and off a number of times, then yell out, 'Lightning, Lightning'.

5. Wait a moment, then run past the stalls, banging your fists on the doors and yelling, 'Thunder, Thunder'.

6. Wait a moment, then pick the bucket up and carry it towards the victim's stall.

7. Yell out, 'Rain, Rain' and throw the water over the top of the stall door.

8. Run as fast as you can. If the victim finds out who you are, you're likely to receive a drenching yourself.

The Artwork

This practical joke is played at an art exhibition at your school.

The Sting

It is the opening of the art exhibition and art lovers are walking around studying the exhibits. They come across a very strange one. It is a blank piece of paper with an ink spot on it. You and a friend are standing in front of this work discussing how good it is and what you think it represents. Gradually, other people also start discussing it. They all have their own ideas of what the painting means. You and your friend stand back and have fun watching and listening to these so-called art experts. The reason for your amusement is that the painting they are discussing was done by you and secretly taped to the wall.

What You Need

- a painting
- some adhesive tape
- a label
- a friend to help with the joke

"PAINTING IN INVISIBLE INK" by I.C. LITTLE

The Set-up

1. Paint a simple picture. The idea of this joke is to get people discussing a work of art that you know has no meaning whatsoever. Here are a few suggestions:

   - an ink spot on white paper

   - a piece of paper with a single piece of string hanging off it

   - a piece of paper with two stripes painted on it

   - a crumpled piece of paper glued to a piece of paper of a different colour

2. Give your work of art a title and write this on the label. The name should be as unusual as the artwork.

3. Make up the name of an artist and write this on the label as well.

4. Take your picture, label and some tape to an art show.

5. When you are alone in the room, quickly tape the painting and label to the wall

near some other pictures. Your friend can act as lookout.

6. Stand in front of your painting and wait for some people to enter the room. As they walk past, start discussing your work of art with your friend. Talk loudly so that people can hear you. Before long, you'll have many people discussing your work.

The Paper Tube

This word joke does not only rely on the words you use. It also relies on what you show the victim.

The Sting

The victim is shown a piece of paper with a tiny hole in the middle of it. They are then asked whether they can push a finger through the centre of the paper without tearing the paper. Of course, they will say it is impossible. When you claim that you can do it, they'll either have a go and fail or they'll say that you can't do it. Then it's your turn to show them exactly how it's done. The trick is in the words that you use. The small hole is just put in the paper to mislead the victim.

What You Need

- paper (preferably more than one piece)
- a pin or pair of scissors

The Set-up

1. Using a pin or a pair of scissors, make a small hole in the middle of a piece of paper. The hole must be big enough to see but small enough not to allow a finger to pass through it.

2. Make a similar hole in another piece of paper. You may need this piece if the victim decides to take up your challenge and tears the other piece.

3. Hold one piece of paper up, showing your victim the hole. Then ask your victim the following question, making sure you use

these exact words: 'Do you think you can push your finger through the centre of the paper without tearing it?'

4. When your victim says it can't be done, or after they've had an attempt and failed, tell them that you can do it.

5. Take the piece of paper and roll it into a tube. Then put your finger into the tube. You are pushing your finger through the centre of the paper without tearing it, just as you said you could.

Bus Stop

This joke doesn't have a victim but it certainly makes the other passengers take notice and gives them something to talk about at work and school. The joke is ideal for a group of drama students.

The Sting

On morning, you get on a bus (or tram or train) and sit down. At the next stop, someone gets on and hands you a tray with the morning newspaper on it. At the next stop, someone gets on with a bunch of flowers for you. At the next stop, someone gets on with a box of chocolates for you. At the next stop, someone gets on and takes a photo of you. By now, the other passengers are staring at you and waiting to see who will get on at the next stop. At the second last stop, someone gets on, wipes your hands and face and takes your tray away. At your last stop, you stand up and get off, as if this happens to you every morning.

What You Need

- lots of volunteers

- a tray

- the morning newspaper

- flowers

- a box of chocolates

- a camera

- a cloth or face washer

The Set-up

1. Work out exactly which person is going to get on at which stop and with which props.

2. Make sure everyone has a copy of the timetable and knows which bus (or tram or train) you are going to be on.

3. The actors should also know exactly where you are going to be sitting.

4. Start the journey and try to blend in with the other passengers.

5. As each actor gets on, act as if it is the most natural thing in the world to be treated like a movie star on public transport. The actors must also be as natural as possible.

15 seconds after the WORLDS BIGGEST BUBBLE GUM BUBBLE RECORD was blown

Set-up Tips

- This practical joke requires the participants to be good actors. The joke works best if everyone acts as if what they are doing is perfectly normal.

- Once the participants have handed you their goods, they should walk away and leave you alone.

- You can add to the joke by getting on the bus in your pyjamas and dressing gown and having some people bring you your clothes during the trip. You can put these clothes on over your pyjamas.

Moth Attack

Moths are attracted to light. Knowing this means you can play this joke at school or at home.

The Sting

Your teacher has planned a special class. You are going to see some slides. Your teacher turns the main light off and switches the projector on. The students pay attention to the screen as the teacher describes the slides. Suddenly something flickers across the screen. It happens again. And again. There are moths loose in the room and they are fluttering about the projector light. Their shadows appear on the screen, causing several students to shriek with fright. The teacher has to give up on the lesson.

What You Need

- a shoebox

- moths

- a dark room with a single light source

The Set-up

1. The day before carrying out this joke, collect some moths. The best way to collect moths is with a net.

2. Keep the moths in a cardboard box, with small holes in the lid, so that they won't die.

3. Take the box of moths to school. Keep the box hidden until the slideshow has been going for a few minutes.

4. When everyone is distracted by what they are watching, take the lid off the box and watch the moths fly straight to the light.

Similar Jokes

*   If your parents are in the habit of holding a slide night after returning from a holiday, then you could liven their show up with this joke. Some of your parents' guests may welcome the distraction.

*   If you have a brother or sister who studies at their desk late at night, sneak into their room when they go to the bathroom or kitchen and set some moths free. When your brother or sister returns, they will find a swarm of moths flying around their desk lamp.

Parking Ticket

Parking Ticket is a joke to play on people with cars. It is particularly amusing if you can be near the victim when they find what they think is a parking ticket.

The Sting

The victim parks their car in a two-hour parking spot. They go off to do some shopping and return after an hour. They put the shopping into the boot of their car and walk around to the front. They stop in horror when they see a parking ticket on their windscreen. They check the words on the parking sign, then check their watch. They can't understand how they got a ticket. By now, they are pretty angry. They rip the ticket off their windscreen and open it up to see how much they have been fined. The ticket reads 'Thank you for parking legally. Have a nice day'.

What You Need

- coloured paper

- sticky tape

- a sheet of plastic

- a parking ticket

The Set-up

1. Have a look at a parking ticket. If someone in your family gets one, ask to have a look. If you can't get hold of a parking ticket, walk down the street and see if you can spot a car with a parking ticket. Don't touch it but notice what colour it is, what

size it is, and how it is folded and taped to the windscreen.

2. Buy some paper the same colour as the parking ticket. Cut it to size and write a message on it. The message should let the driver know they have been the victim of a practical joke.

3. Fold the paper to the right size.

4. You may want to wrap the ticket in plastic before taping it to a windscreen.

5. Go to a busy street where there are parking restrictions and put the ticket on the windscreen of a parked car. Make sure the driver does not see you.

A little too much of that IRON enriched breakfast cereal

6. Wait nearby and watch the reaction of the victim when they return to their car. Most people are pretty angry when they get a parking ticket, especially when they know they have done nothing wrong.

7. Watch if their reaction changes when they read the message you wrote.

Ghost Story

Hearing a ghost story can be scary enough. Imagine how scary it can be if ghosts seem to appear.

The Sting

A group of your friends are sitting around while you tell a ghost story. The story is frightening, and every now and again strange sounds can be heard. At first, these sounds are very faint and no one says anything because they think they might be imagining it. However, when furniture starts to move, everyone starts screaming. Only you know the truth. You have to decide whether to let your friends in on the joke or let them believe they really saw and heard ghosts.

What You Need

- friends to help you carry out the joke
- pebbles
- torches
- fishing line
- a tape recorder
- a blank audiotape

The Set-up

The planning for this joke starts well before you begin telling your ghost story. You have to organise one group of friends to play a few tricks while you're telling another group of friends a ghost story. Below are a few tricks the first group of friends can help you play. Use your imagination and come up with ideas of your own.

1. A friend can throw small pebbles against the outside of the window of the room you're in. Try and arrange for it to happen at a point in your story when you talk about a ghost tapping on the window.

2. A friend can shine a torch outside the window at a point in your story when you talk about strange lights being seen. If the light inside is off, the light being shone outside will stand out more.

3. During the day, tie some fishing line to a couple of objects in the room where you'll be telling the story. During the story, a friend can pull the end of the fishing line from under the doorframe or an open window. It will appear as if the objects are moving on their own.

4. If you don't have anyone to help you play tricks, you can still do it yourself. Use a tape recorder to record some scary noises on an audiotape. Set the tape recorder up

somewhere in the house. Before starting the ghost story, press the 'Play' button. You should have about fifteen minutes of silence on the audiotape, and then the strange noises should begin. The scary noises should only be heard every now and again.

Sore Neck

Sore Neck is not so much a scary joke but one that will make people feel pretty sick. The success of this joke depends a great deal on your ability as an actor.

The Sting

You are sitting next to your victim. You complain that you have a sore neck. A few minutes later, you complain again. This time, you ask the victim to gently massage the back of your neck. The victim does, but the massage doesn't seem to do any good. A couple of minutes later, you grab your head and turn it sharply to the side. The movement is accompanied by a loud cracking sound that makes the victim cry out. You simply shake your head a couple of times and smile, as if you feel much better.

What You Need

- a plastic cup

The Set-up

1. This joke works best on a long bus trip.

2. Make sure you are sitting next to your victim.

3. After a while, complain about having a sore neck and shake it from side to side a couple of times. (Do this gently; you don't really want to hurt your neck.)

4. A few minutes later, complain that your neck is still sore and ask the victim to give your neck a quick massage. It doesn't really matter if the victim agrees to massage your neck or not. It's just a good

way to mention your neck again and build up the joke.

5. A few minutes later, complain again about your neck. Tell the victim that you're going to try to snap your neck back into place.

6. Without the victim seeing, place the plastic cup between your body and upper arm.

7. Grab your head with both hands. Breathe heavily a few times as if you are bracing yourself for something painful.

WHOA!
Who greased the slide..?

8. Twist your head to the side, while dropping your arm hard against the plastic cup. The cup should crush and make a loud cracking sound.

9. Sigh in relief, then smile at your victim. They'll probably be as white as a sheet believing that you've cracked the bones in your neck.

10. You should practise the twisting and crushing movement a few times at home, as the timing is very important.

My Left Elbow

For this joke to work, you must say the crucial words exactly as they are written in the Set-up section.

The Sting

You tell the victim that you can write with your left elbow. Of course they won't believe you. You insist that it is possible and that they should have a try. They may try to balance the pen on their elbow and then write, but they'll probably just tell you that it's impossible. You tell them that you'll show them how it's done if they'll polish your shoes for a month. When they agree, you do exactly as you said you would. You write with your left elbow.

What You Need

- a piece of paper

- a pen

The Set-up

1. Put a pen and a piece of paper in front of your victim.

2. Say the following words exactly: 'I can write with my left elbow'. After you have said those words, you might like to add something like, 'I bet you can't do it' or 'Will you buy me an ice cream if I can do it?'

3. When your victim says it can't be done, or after they've had an attempt and failed, tell them you'll show them how.

4. Roll up your sleeve and try to balance the pen on your left elbow. You can even get

a cloth out and rub your elbow in preparation. It doesn't matter what you do to your elbow because you're not actually going to use it. It is just part of the act.

5. Grab the pen in your hand and write the following words on the piece of paper: 'with my left elbow'.

6. Show the piece of paper to your friend and say, 'See, I told you that I could write *with my left elbow.*'

Feeling Sick

If this joke doesn't make the person sitting next to you feel sick, then there's something very wrong with them. It's a great joke to play on long car trips.

The Sting

The victim is on a long car trip. They just want the trip to be over. Suddenly, the person sitting next to them grabs a paper bag and vomits into it. They then wipe their face and lean back, holding onto the bag. A few minutes later, the sick person appears to be feeling better. The victim looks on with

shock and disgust as the sick person grabs
a spoon, opens the bag and begins to eat the
contents.

What You Need

- a paper bag

- a can of creamed corn (or other chunky
  food stuff)

- a spoon

The Set-up

1. Before the car trip begins, or when your
   victim is away from their seat, tip the
   contents of the can into the paper bag.

2. At some point in the trip, mention to the
   victim that you are feeling a bit sick.

3. A few minutes later, moan a little bit.

4. A few minutes later, grab the paper bag,
   lurch forward in your seat and pretend to
   vomit into the bag.

5. Sit back and wipe your mouth.

6. A few minutes later, apologise to the victim and tell them you are feeling better.

7. Grab a spoon, open the bag and begin to eat the contents.

8. If you want to gross the victim out even more, offer them a spoonful.